Jed's ...

Ant...

Illustrated by Tim Beer

ONE

"We're stranded," said Debbie gloomily, looking up and down the creek that was all too obviously drying out fast. Debbie had been teaching Jack and Laura to sail on *The Flying Dutchman*, but now the old wooden sailing cruiser was firmly stuck in the mud.

"Can't we swim for it?" asked Laura.

"You'd never manage against the tide," replied Debbie. "It's running out too quickly."

She's right, thought Jack. The muddy brown water was swirling away at an incredible rate and he knew that if they attempted to swim they would be carried out to sea in a few minutes.

"As your instructor, I feel a bit of a fool," admitted Debbie with a faint grin. She was small and neat and efficient, with an elfin face that was always warm and sympathetic. Not the kind of person to make mistakes, thought Laura, but definitely the kind of person to admit to them if she did.

"You couldn't help the engine giving us trouble," said Jack. "It could have happened to anyone."

There was a long silence, finally broken by Laura. "How long are we going to be here?" she asked.

Debbie's grin widened. "I was waiting for someone to ask me that. About another four hours at least, I'd reckon."

"Blimey!" said Jack.

"There's plenty of food down below, and we could play cards."

Laura cheered up. "This could be fun," she said.

The other two looked at her doubtfully.

"Won't they be worried about us at the Adventure Centre?" asked Jack.

"I've radioed them. They know when to expect us." Debbie sighed. "It's a good thing you were the only two who wanted to come out tonight. We might have been stuck with some of the younger kids – the over-active ones."

Laura looked around at the summer evening shadows on the creek and the sun going down on the estuary beyond. "I love it out here – it's so peaceful."

"What are we missing at the centre?" asked Jack sadly. "Wasn't there going to be a five-a-side football competition? I wanted to be in that."

"Well – you're not," said his young sister crossly. "So make the best of it."

"I didn't say I wasn't going to, did I, bossy?"

Debbie left them to squabble and went down to the cabin to make some hot chocolate. She liked Jack and Laura a lot, more than any of the other kids who had come all the way from their London primary school for a week at the Old Vicarage Adventure Centre. Laura was one of the most determined girls she had ever met, much more serious-minded than her elder brother Jack, who was happy-go-lucky, spontaneous and slapdash.

As she made the chocolate, Debbie's mind reluctantly turned to darker thoughts. Would *he* make it back tonight? Would he be able to swim against the tide this time or would she see him sink below the waves yet again?

The setting sun was just dipping into the sea in a flush of crimson when Jack said suddenly, "There's a ship."

"Where?" Laura had been watching a skein of geese wheeling up into the darkening sky.

"And *what* a ship!" whispered Jack.

She saw it at once, silhouetted against the skyline. "It's an old barge," she said.

"And it's in trouble," breathed Jack.

Suddenly all hell broke loose on the estuary behind them. They watched in stunned, bewildered, horrified amazement for while the creek remained windless the estuary was a crackling inferno of massive waves, sheets of lightning and great growling roars of thunder. It was unbelievable.

Worse was to follow, as wave after wave struck the sailing barge with tremendous force. A mast went down with a rending and tearing of wood, a sail split from top to bottom, and then slowly and relentlessly the barge began to turn on to its side.

"I don't believe it," muttered Jack.

"How can a storm be out there when it's calm here?" whispered Laura.

Out in the estuary, the wild weather continued, the wind screaming and the waves lashing at the sides of the stricken barge. Then Jack saw the boy's head bobbing in the water.

TWO

"Look, he's drowning," said Laura. "He'll never make it to the creek. I'm going after him."

"No, the tide's too strong!" yelled Jack, grabbing her arm.

"He's going under." She struggled to release herself.

"So will you! You'll drown!"

"Get off."

But Jack hung on and, as he was physically the stronger of the two, Laura was trapped.

"I said – get off!" she yelled furiously, determined not to give up.

"Debbie," shouted Jack. "Debbie – help me!"

With a wild swing of her fist, Laura caught Jack round the side of the head and he fell back with a howl of pain, releasing her arm. In seconds, well before Debbie had managed to run up from the cabin, Laura had dived over the side of *The Flying Dutchman* into the swirling tide below.

"What's happening?" asked Debbie. "What's all the shouting?" She stared around the deck, her eyes suddenly dilating with a dreadful realisation.

"Where's Laura?"

But Jack wasn't there any longer. He was diving off the side to join his sister in the flurry of the tide.

As he surfaced, Jack looked ahead towards the estuary, but the storm wasn't there any longer. The water was calm and the capsized barge and the struggling boy had disappeared.

Then he didn't have time to think for he could feel the deadly pull of the tide sweeping him out to sea.

"Laura," he screamed, and swallowed water. "Laura!"

Behind him, there was another splash as Debbie dived off the deck of *The Flying Dutchman*. Thank God we're all wearing life-jackets, she thought, wincing as she felt the pull of the tide. They were all going to be swept out to sea. Why had Laura jumped over the side? Why?

"Laura!" cried Jack, and swallowed more water. "Laura, where are you?" The tide swept him on, past high mud banks, past a field of grazing cattle and then in greater strength past a pebble beach. "Laura!" he called despairingly. "Where are you, Laura?"

There was less of a drag now that he was out at sea. "Laura!" A few motor boats at anchor bobbed up and down, miserably empty, affording no assistance. But what was that, he wondered, clinging to an anchor chain in the twilight? Was it a figure? Was it Laura? Please God, let it be Laura.

Debbie swam on, trying to keep Jack's bobbing head in view, knowing that it reminded her of another bobbing head – one that she never seemed able to reach. Suppose they drowned? Suppose she couldn't save Jack and Laura? And why oh why had Laura gone overboard?

It was Laura. It really was her, clinging to the weed-heavy chain. Using up his last ounce of strength, Jack managed to reach her.
"Laura!"
"I'm sorry!" She was gasping for breath. "I thought you'd drowned."

"I'm OK. You did see him, didn't you?"

"The boy in the water, you mean? Yes, I saw him."

"And now he's gone," she said in a weak thread of a voice. "It's all gone. The storm, the barge – everything."

"Don't keep talking – don't keep tiring yourself out." He clung to the chain as well, treading water, supporting his sister's head.

"You did see it, didn't you? You did see it all?"

"I saw it."

"And now it's gone! Jack, what did we see? What does it mean?"

"I don't know. Hang on tight. Look, Debbie's coming."

"She'll be furious!" said Laura weakly. "Absolutely furious."

Debbie was just that. "What on earth do you think you're both doing?" she gasped. "Are you crazy?"

"We saw a ship going down," spluttered Laura. "In a storm – and a boy swimming away."

They were all three hanging on to the slimy anchor chain now and Jack took a look at Debbie's face. Was it grey with exhaustion, or could it be fear?

THREE

"What did you say?"

"I said there was a storm and a ship. An old sailing barge capsized, and there was a boy swimming away. He was drowning. I had to help him. Jack saw it too, didn't you?"

"Yes, I saw it."

Debbie said nothing, but there was shock written all over her face. "What's the matter, Debbie?" he asked.

"Nothing."

"But –"

"Nothing. We can't have a conversation out here. We'll all suffer from exposure." She looked desperately around and was relieved to catch sight of a motor-boat. "Ahoy," she yelled. "Ahoy there! Come on, you two, shout – unless you want to spend the night hanging on to this anchor chain."

The motor-boat changed direction and came their way, but it seemed like an eternity before it finally arrived.

"Out for a swim?" said the helmsman, throttling back his engine.

"Rather a long one," replied Debbie. "Could you take us back to our boat? It's *The Flying Dutchman*."

"Where is she?"

"On a mud bank in the creek. We missed the tide because of engine trouble."

"What are you doing out here?" he asked. Then the helmsman obviously decided that he was not exactly minding his own business. "Come on then." He passed Debbie an oar. "Grab this and I'll pull you in."

Debbie, Jack and Laura finally had their hot chocolate after their rescuer had dropped them off on the *Dutchman*. They were silent, hunched in blankets and reflecting on what had happened. Then Laura said suddenly, "We did see it all, Debbie."

Debbie shook her head impatiently. "It must have been a trick of the light."

"How could it have been?" said Jack angrily. "We're not idiots."

Despite the warmth of the little galley, he shivered, feeling strangely apprehensive and tense. "You've *got* to believe us."

"I do," said Debbie, not meeting his eyes. "You did see something but it *was* a trick of the light. Out here, the effects are very odd and – "

"Debbie," said Laura quietly.

"Yes?" Debbie's voice had an edge to it.

"You've seen it too, haven't you?"

"What do you mean?"

"The storm, the barge – and that drowning boy."

There was a long silence, and then Debbie said with a catch in her voice, "Yes – I've seen him. And I don't know what to do."

FOUR

Laura put her arm round Debbie while Jack still sat awkwardly in his blanket.

"Don't cry, Debbie."

"I'm sorry – I thought you'd drowned."

"So did I!" said Jack with feeling.

"Well I didn't. I *had* to help him. Haven't you ever wanted to do that?"

"Yes, of course I have!"

"But *did* you?" asked Jack stolidly.

"Yes, I swam with the tide as well. But it all disappeared – just like it did with you. *He* disappeared."

"So what is he?" asked Jack. "What is it all?"

"Are they – is he a ghost?" asked Laura.

"Yes," said Debbie slowly. "I think he must be."

When the tide finally turned, *The Flying Dutchman* slipped off her mud bank and they floated slowly back to the Old Vicarage Adventure Centre where they were all greeted with derisive shouts and much wearisome teasing. It was past eleven and Jack and Laura were soon in bed, physically exhausted but with their minds racing.

"What happened?" asked Chris, Jack's best friend, who slept next to him in the dormitory.

"Not a lot. We got stuck on a mud bank, that's all. Engine trouble."

"How come your clothes were all wet? Did you get out and push?"

"Something like that," sighed Jack and pretended to be asleep, but directly he closed his eyes he saw the boy's head again, disappearing under the waves.

"How come all your clothes got wet then?" asked Tracy, who slept in the next bed to Laura in the girls' dormitory.

"We got out and pushed, didn't we?" she snapped, and turned her back on her inquisitive neighbour, pretending to be asleep, and giving vent to a large snore to keep the questions at bay. Through tightly shut eyes Laura saw the boy going under the waves. Who was he, she wondered. Did Debbie know any more than she was letting on? Eventually she dozed off, only to dream of a dark head in the sea and she herself swimming desperately towards it – but never getting there.

Something woke Jack, but he wasn't sure what it was. He thought he'd heard someone calling outside, but the voice could have been part of his dreams. Then he heard the sound again.

Quickly, making sure the others were still asleep, Jack got out of bed and stole cautiously to the window. When he looked out, he received a terrible shock.

FIVE

Debbie was standing on the path by the creek. Behind her was the sailing dinghy and canoe park and further along, to the right of the overgrown orchard, was a collection of sheds, the climbing wall and a mobile classroom.

The moon shone brightly overhead, picking out the detail in the buildings. Everything was normal, except for the now familiar dark head that was bobbing up and down in the creek.

Then he heard Debbie calling out a name – and he recognised it as the sound that had awoken him.

"Jed," she was calling. "Oh please, Jed, it's only another few metres. You've never been so near before. Just push on a bit." The dark head looked up at her and in the

moonlight Jack could see a pale, washed-out face and huge, exhausted, fearful eyes.

"It's not far now – you've broken through – they won't get you now. You're safe – safe to come home."

Her voice was very clear in the still night and Jack could hear every word. Then, quite suddenly and without any warning at all, the dark head disappeared under the water and didn't come up again.

Debbie stood on the towpath, staring unbelievingly down at the creek. "Jed," she called as loudly as she dared. "Jed – you're almost home. Don't give up now."

But the water in the creek flowed on and there was no longer any sign of a dark head. Debbie began to sob and Jack longed to do something to comfort her. But what? He felt completely helpless as he watched her walk slowly back into the house.

Even when Debbie had disappeared inside, Jack still stayed at the window, watching the creek, hoping for the reappearance of Jed.

Suddenly a shadow detached itself from the wall and he saw Laura walking towards the creek.

He watched her intently. There was something about the *way* she was walking that immediately worried him – something about her slow methodical steps. Could she be sleep-walking? In seconds, Jack realised that she was, and that in front of her the bobbing black head had reappeared in the water – and this time an arm was visible, waving and beckoning to his sister.

Jack was down on the ground floor and had noiselessly unlocked the front door in a flash, but when he reached the towpath he gasped in horror, wondering if he was already too late. Laura was kneeling by the creek in her pyjamas, holding out her hands to Jed – and he, with a look of great yearning, was treading water and holding out a hand to her.

"Laura!"

She didn't turn, and Jack saw their hands clasp.

"Laura!"

Still she didn't turn and he sprinted towards her, a wave of total panic surging through him. Any moment he could imagine Jed pulling her in and down, down to some watery grave.

"Laura!"

There was still no response, and as he was now within centimetres of her, Jack hurled himself at his sister and she fell backwards with a great thump, with him on top of her. Twisting round to see what had happened to Jed, he caught sight of his face in the water. Immediately he was dazed by the full force of the hatred that radiated from him. Then Jed's head disappeared abruptly from view.

Looking startled, Laura sat up, the first hint of panic beginning to show in her eyes. "What's happening?"

"You're sleep-walking."

She nodded. "But there's something else, isn't there? Someone else."

"There's always Jed."

"What do you mean?"

"The drowning boy. He was waiting in the water for you," Jack said grimly. "Reaching out for you."

Laura looked terrified. "But this could happen again," she stammered.

Jack didn't reply immediately. He didn't know what to say, for the idea of this happening again – and his not being there – was too awful to contemplate. Then he had an idea.

"Debbie," he muttered.

"What do you mean?"

"She knows more than she's letting on. I'm sure she does."

"We'll ask her now," said Laura, yawning and shivering at the same time. "She's just coming out of the centre."

SIX

Very quickly, Jack told Debbie what had happened. She was horrified.

"I felt Jed's presence," she said quietly. "That's why I came out."

"Debbie – " Laura was hesitant. "We think you know more about Jed than you've let on. Can't you tell us a bit more?"

"Now this has happened I will." She looked up to see the first streaks of dawn appearing in the night sky. "Let's walk on a bit and I'll tell you what I know."

"The fact is," began Debbie, "that I deliberately chose the Old Vicarage Adventure Centre to work in. I waited for a long time for a vacancy to occur, and the reason is that my great-great-grandfather – his name was Edward Fox – was the vicar here. The church is in the village but the vicarage was right out here by the creek. This was very convenient, because as well as being a vicar he was also a smuggler."

"Wow!" said Jack. "What kind of things did he smuggle?"

"Mainly silk and perfume from France – brandy too, I think. He had an old barge."

"I see," breathed Laura.

"And a son named Jed."

"What happened?" asked Jack quietly.

"Well, as far as I can see by looking up the old newspapers of the time, the Reverend Fox had a rival – a man named Ralph Appelby, who also went in for smuggling in an old gaffe-rigged schooner called the *Isabella*. They'd fallen out over some deal or other and Appelby swore vengeance. But as it turned out he didn't have to do anything, for the Rose – the Reverend Fox's barge – went down in a storm and the only survivor was Jed. But he didn't survive for long."

She paused and both Laura and Jack could see that she was finding it hard to continue. "He managed to swim as far as the *Isabella* which was moored at the mouth of the creek, taking shelter from the storm." Her voice broke. "Jed tried to clamber on board but Appelby pushed him off again and again and again." She paused again, hardly able to control the anguish in her voice. "In despair Jed tried to swim up the creek towards home, but every time he tried to scramble up the bank, Ralph Appelby pushed him back again. No doubt he thought it was great sport."

"What happened in the end?" whispered Laura.

"Jed drowned. He never got home to the vicarage."

There was a long, long pause. Then Jack asked uneasily, "Debbie. How do you know all this? Did you read it in the old newspapers?"

She shook her head. "No – Jed told me."

SEVEN

"What?" Laura stared at Debbie as if she had gone completely crazy.

"Yes," replied Debbie patiently. "Jed told me." She seemed completely calm now and very rational.

"How did he tell you?" asked Jack incredulously.

"Ever since I came here he's been trying to reach me. I kept seeing the vision of the ship sinking and Jed swimming. Then I saw him further up the creek, trying to get home. Worse still, I've seen things you haven't seen – terrible things."

"Ralph Appelby – and what he did to Jed?" asked Jack.

"Yes. I can't bear even to think about it – let alone see it. Then I caught sight of him, hanging on to a piece of wood in the creek. I tried to pull him out, but of course I couldn't reach him."

"So that's what he wanted," said Jack slowly. "For Laura to pull him out. He wasn't trying to pull *her* in."

"No. Jed is lost and lonely and desperate, but he's not evil like Appelby. Anyway, clinging to his plank – he told me what had happened. He didn't exactly speak. This voice came into my head and I knew it was him – knew he was telling the truth. Then the tide turned." She began to cry. "And do you know – do you know – it took him back out to sea. That's what it does – that's what it will do. Forever."

Laura put her arm round Debbie's heaving shoulders and Jack watched them, not self-conscious and embarrassed but deeply, deeply moved.

After a while Debbie felt strong enough to carry on.

"There's something else," she said, "something awful. Something that Jed told me."

"Tell us," said Jack, trying to sound as confident and reassuring as he could. But when he saw Debbie's terrified face a chill crept over him.

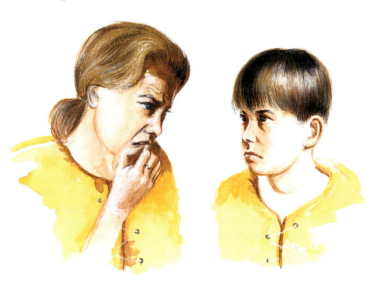

"He told me how much Ralph Appelby hated my family – how his curse had lasted from generation to generation. Terrible things happened after Appelby died: two of my ancestors, two children, drowned in the creek, and there were other drownings. My uncle and an old aunt were drowned at sea."

"It could have all been a coincidence," reasoned Jack uneasily.

"Not according to Jed. Appelby wants to destroy my family, or at least destroy as many members of it as he can. And now he's trying to destroy me."

"What?" Laura was horrified.

"How?" asked Jack baldly. He wished he could dismiss Debbie's fears as ridiculous, but somehow he knew he couldn't.

"I nearly drowned when I tried to rescue Jed the first time, and I fell off a sailing dinghy when I was with a group, right out at sea. There was no reason to fall like that. I've been sailing for years."

"Were you pushed?" asked Jack.

"I just fell," replied Debbie, her eyes alight with fear as she looked into the dark water of the creek.

"Debbie, why did you want to come back to the Old Vicarage?" asked Laura gently.

"I don't know. I was desperate to come. Maybe Jed was calling me."

"But we've seen Jed too," said Laura. "What does that mean, Debbie?"

"I don't know."

"Has anyone else ever seen him?"

"No," Debbie replied flatly. "Not to my knowledge."

"Then he must want us to help him too," said Jack.

EIGHT

"If you try to help Jed, you'll come up against Appelby," whispered Debbie.

"We want to help Jed, but we want to help you too," said Jack.

"After all," put in Laura, "Jed's a ghost and you're alive."

"I won't be much longer if Appelby has anything to do with it." Her voice was so faint that they could only just make out what she was saying.

"We won't let him touch you," said Jack grimly.

Debbie tried to pull herself together and she looked quickly down at her watch. "It's almost five. You *must* get some sleep." She paused. "I feel so bad – so impossible – talking to you like this. You're so young and –"

"Listen, Debbie," said Laura. "We may be young, but don't talk down to us. We'll help you – and Jed too."

"The question is," said Jack, "what's the plan of action?"

"I've got an idea." Laura's voice was determined. "But I'm not sure if it's going to work."

"Well?" Debbie looked at her hopefully.

"If we can only get Jed home – home to the vicarage – won't that show Appelby his power's on the wane? It might even put paid to him completely."

"Brilliant. That'll sort them both out," said Jack, but inwardly he felt very apprehensive. He still didn't trust Jed, still remembered the look of hate he had given him from the water.

"It's no guarantee," said Debbie sadly.

"And I've tried to help him home."

"I think Laura could," said Jack, feeling very uneasy. "But I'm not sure I want her to."

"Why not?" Laura snapped.

"You ought to have seen that look he had on his face when he saw me – pure hatred."

"Maybe he thought you were something to do with Ralph Appelby," suggested Debbie.

"Is there anything else we should know before we put our plan into operation?" asked Laura.

"Maybe one thing," said Debbie. "But I still reckon I'm being desperately irresponsible, dragging you into all this."

"And *we* say you're being dead patronising," protested Laura fiercely. "Now what were you going to say?"

"The *Isabella* – Ralph Appelby's boat – she's at the top of the creek."

"What!" exclaimed Jack.

"She's a hulk – just a dried-out hulk – but she's the *Isabella* sure enough."

There was a long silence. Then Laura said, "What are we doing today?"

"Canoeing with George. It's my day off."

"Why don't we go sick?" said Jack. "Then we can all three go and explore the *Isabella*."

"You'd never convince that teacher of yours," replied Debbie. "It'll look too suspicious if you both go sick. Tell you what though – aren't you both experienced canoeists anyway?"

"Yes," said Laura. "We've been on a white water course, and we've got our own canoes on the Thames."

"And the others are all beginners."

Debbie grinned for the first time and winked at them as if they were conspirators.

"Yes," said Laura, smiling back at her.

"OK. I'll tell George I'm going to take you on a canoe journey while he gives the others the beginners' course. I just hope it won't look too much like favouritism – " Her voice tailed away doubtfully.

"It won't," said Jack. "Besides, there's too much at stake to worry about things like that."

In the end, they only had about three hours sleep, but both Jack and Laura plunged into it immediately and, surprisingly, woke after their night-time's experiences feeling quite refreshed. No one suspected anything over breakfast, although there was some bad feeling when

Debbie came over to their table and gave them a thumbs-up sign.

"What does that mean?" asked Len Nutwood suspiciously. He was always on the watch for being left out.

"We've done so much canoeing in the past that we've got our certificates and everything," said Jack with studied casualness. "So we're going out with Debbie for some practice and then we'll join you in the next session." He tried hard not to sound superior but already Len was looking aggrieved.

"That's good of you," he said unpleasantly. "You fancy Debbie or something? You're getting really thick with her, aren't you?"

"Honestly," said Laura, trying not to be annoyed. "It's nothing to do with that – it's just we've got our own canoes and – "

"Lucky you," snarled Len. "I suppose you reckon the rest of us are real plebs – "

"Why don't I alter your face a little bit after breakfast?" Jack was often aggressive and had little patience.

Laura winced. This was the last thing she wanted. But she'd reckoned without Len's cowardice.

"All right," he sneered. "Can't you take a joke?"

"Not your kind," replied Jack sharply, but Laura was relieved to see that he seemed content to leave it at that.

"Here we are," said Debbie, "the *Isabella* – at last."

They had paddled about a mile up the creek which gradually narrowed off between grassy banks. Both Jack and Laura noticed that Debbie was exhausted this morning, and there was a hunted look in her eyes that neither of them liked.

The *Isabella* was certainly a hulk – a boat-shaped lump of rotting wood halfway up a mud bank with her keel half eaten away and no masts or rigging at all.

Jack felt flat as he paddled his canoe up to her. It was a bright, warm morning with the sun high in the sky and the very thought of ghosts or supernatural influences seemed ludicrous. You couldn't have ghosts in sunlight, he thought. They belonged to the twilight, to mist and fog, to night, to dark silent woods or ruined, sombre buildings.

Then Jack paddled round to the dark side of the hulk – the section that was in shadow – and he wasn't so sure. Very dimly he could make out the carved name *Isabella*. He shivered. It was cold here and

he wanted to paddle back into the sun.
The water was greeny-grey and gloomy
looking, and for a moment he stared
down into it, puzzled at a shape or
shadow he couldn't quite make out. Then
the chill inside his stomach became blind
panic, and with a scream of fear Jack
overturned his canoe.

For seconds – maybe a minute – he splashed around, yelling his head off until Debbie and Laura came to him, paddling fast.

Laura started to laugh and then stopped when she saw her brother's horrified face. Debbie, who couldn't see him properly, said teasingly, "And there I was thinking you were an experienced canoeist – " Then she too saw Jack's face. "What on earth's the matter?"

"Get me out," he shrieked. "Get me out of here."

"Climb up the bank!" shouted Laura. "It's only a few metres. Swim for it. Go for it – now! We'll take care of the canoe."

Splashing madly, Jack set off towards the muddy shore and then scrambled up it as if there was something hideous and menacing behind him. Perhaps there was, thought Laura suddenly, and stared down into the water. But all she could see was the cloudy surface.

As she and Laura towed in Jack's canoe, Debbie said very calmly and soothingly, "What did you see?"

Jack didn't answer immediately. He just sat there, his head clasped in his hands. Then he looked down at them and they saw that the terror was still in his eyes.

"I saw this guy."

"In the water?" asked Laura.

"Yeah – just below the surface. He was kind of floating, looking up at me with this horrible smile."

"What did he look like?" said Debbie quietly.

"Very thin – with a moustache and – kind of hollow eyes."

"How was he dressed?"

"Sort of weird – thick white shirt – frills all down the front and flopping over his hands."

"You were looking at Ralph Appelby," said Debbie woodenly.

NINE

"What was he doing?" asked Laura.

"Making himself known to Jack," said Debbie. "I've – he's already very familiar to me."

"Do you think he'll – he'll make himself known to me too?" asked Laura, looking scared.

"I expect so. I don't know."

"I'm sorry to have panicked like that." Jack was ashamed now. "It was just such an awful shock."

"I can understand that." Debbie's voice was faint. Then she tried to smile. "Do you want to go on board?" she said with an attempt at briskness.

"Can you?" asked Jack. "I mean – she's falling to pieces."

"Not completely," said Debbie. "Come

on, I'll show you. But tread carefully. She's rotten through and through."

"Like her owner," pointed out Laura sharply.

Once they were all on the bank and cautiously climbing on to what was left of the *Isabella's* decks, Jack felt a great deal better. But the cruel, knowing smile on Ralph Appelby's face stayed in his mind and he was sure he would remember it all his life.

"There's only one way down and there's no ladder, so take care," said Debbie.

"You've been here before?" asked Laura.

"Yes."

"On your own?"

Debbie nodded, and Laura took her arm affectionately. "I do think you've got guts."

Debbie frowned. "It's got nothing to do with that. It's Jed. I must help him. Come on, follow me."

They dropped down into a dark cavernous space, where there was complete silence except for the sound of lapping water outside.

"What is this?" asked Laura.

"The hold, but there's a couple of cabins left forward. Keep together."

"Was one of those cabins his, do you reckon?"

Debbie shrugged. "I don't know. I have to say I've never seen any ghosts down here. But that doesn't mean anything – "

"Where *have* you seen him then?"

"On the path by the side of the creek. Several times."

"And what's he been doing?" asked Jack.

"Laughing. Enjoying himself. Watching Jed drown – like he's watched him on every tide, every day of every year, for so long."

There were no doors to the cabins – just more rotten wood and what looked as if it could have been a bunk.

"Listen!" said Laura suddenly.

"I can't hear anything," said Jack.

"Neither can I." Debbie was listening very intently.

"You must be able to," Laura replied impatiently. "You must. Listen!"

But the other two couldn't hear anything.

To Laura, the footsteps seemed thunderous, and they were marching across the deck, down towards the drop to the hold.

"He's coming," whispered Laura.

"Who's coming?"

"Ralph. Ralph Appelby. I can hear his footsteps." Laura's voice was rising hysterically.

"I can't hear anything," repeated Jack but Laura put a finger to her lips. She stood there, straining her ears, but the footsteps had stopped and there was total silence, except for the lapping of the water outside. And that was somehow very much worse.

"What's the matter?" asked Debbie tensely.

"They've stopped."

"Great," said Jack, slightly impatiently.

"He's waiting."

"*What?*"

"He's waiting up there."

"I'll go," said Debbie.

"No – I will." But Jack's voice had a tremble in it.

"It won't take me a sec." Before either of them could argue, she had swung herself up on to the crumbling deck.

The silence intensified.

"I can't hear her footsteps now," whimpered Laura.

"That deck   it's all damp and soft. You wouldn't hear anyone's footsteps."

"I heard his," she retorted.

"But – " Suddenly Jack didn't want to argue any longer. "What are we doing standing here? Why don't we go and join her?"

Together, they ran towards the gap in the deck – and the silence above them.

She wasn't there, and when they looked over at the banks, the canoes, the fields beyond – she wasn't there either.

"This is ridiculous," said Jack.

Laura said nothing and he looked at her fearfully for she was scanning the water, her eyes intent – not as if she was looking for Debbie, but as if she was yearning for Jed. The thought raced about in Jack's head, making him deeply uneasy.

"She must be somewhere," he said, desperate to attract her attention, but still Laura didn't reply.

"Laura!"

"Mm?"

"You're not looking for Debbie."

Laura came to abruptly and her eyes darted around anxiously. Suddenly she plunged forward.

"What's up?"

"She's there."

"Where?"

"In the water."

He couldn't understand why he hadn't noticed before. Debbie was floating face down by the canoes.

TEN

Without a word Laura and Jack dived simultaneously into the creek and, within seconds, had grabbed Debbie and heaved her over on to her back. They pulled her in, her life-jacket holding her up, and then dragged her on to the muddy foreshore.

"Is she OK?" asked Jack urgently.

"I think so. She's breathing, but she's probably swallowed a lot of water." Laura began to apply the artificial resuscitation techniques that she had learnt on a life-saving course, and it wasn't long before the water was pumping out of Debbie's lungs.

Soon she was sitting up, coughing but fully conscious.

"What happened?" asked Jack when she seemed a little better.

Still dazed she shook her head and muttered, "I don't know. I must have slipped."

"Or were you pushed?" asked Laura softly.

Debbie stared at them blankly. "I just don't know. I remember coming up on deck and there was no one there – no one there at all. Then the next thing I knew you were pumping me out – for which many thanks." She smiled up at them. "In fact – you two saved my life."

Jack looked around him. He suddenly felt absolutely starving. "Shouldn't we get back to the centre?" he asked. "You need to go to a doctor."

"Rubbish," said Debbie. "I'll be fine. We'll have the sandwiches we brought and then take another look round." She turned to Laura. "Laura – whatever's the matter?"

Jack turned sharply and saw that his sister was cowering in the grass, her eyes fixed on the deck of the Isabella.

"What's up?" asked Jack.
But she gave no reply, her eyes still riveted on the deck.

"Laura!"

"He's there," she whispered.

"Appelby?"

"He's standing on the deck. He's smiling at me."

"Is that all?" asked Debbie.

"Yes – just smiling. That's all." Laura suddenly began to laugh. It wasn't hysterical laughter, but it was the oddest kind of laughter Jack had ever heard, and when he glanced at Debbie he could see she was terrified.

"Shut up, Laura!"

The laughter wasn't hers. It was deep and rich and horrible. Then it stopped, and a voice came out of Laura's mouth that wasn't hers either. "He's mine – the boy's mine. He'll never come home. He'll always stay drowned. You'll never get him home. He'll swim on forever, will Jed. Jed will swim on for eternity." The laughter resumed and then suddenly stopped as if it had been switched off.

Laura stood up, looking at them blankly, and it was some minutes before her eyes began to focus again. She's come back, Jack thought. But where's she been?

"What's happened?" asked Laura.

"You were speaking in a man's voice," Jack said. "He was talking through you. Appelby was using you."

"What was he saying?"

"That Jed wouldn't ever stop swimming – that he'd go on for eternity."

But Laura was immediately positive – positive and angry. "How dare that horrible man use me like that? How dare he! Of course we'll get Jed home."

"Laura – "

"What is it, Jack?"

"You were looking at the water earlier. What did you see?"

"Appelby. At least – I thought I saw the reflection of a man. But maybe I didn't. It was indistinct. I think my imagination's playing tricks – I don't need to see him, do I, Debbie? He can use me any time he likes."

"No," said Debbie forcefully. "He'll never use you again – not if we get Jed home tonight."

"But how?" asked Jack desperately. "How on earth can we do it?"

"I've got an idea," said Laura. Then she paused. "Or don't you trust me? Do you think Appelby's speaking through me – even now?"

"No," said Debbie. "I don't think that. We'd know if he was."

"Yes," said Jack. "We'd definitely know. What's your idea?"

"What time is high tide tonight?" Laura asked Debbie.

"About eight."

"Let's swim with him," said Laura. "We're both about his age, we're both strong swimmers, and the tide will be with us. We can protect him. And it's not that far from the estuary to the vicarage. We should make it before the tide turns. What do you think?"

"Swim and protect him?" mused Jack. "Sounds a great idea. You'll swim too, won't you, Debbie?"

"Of course I will. The only thing is – "

"What?" asked Jack gently.

"It's so dangerous. But – all right, we'll do it." She paused. "I'll tell you what – I've got a brilliant idea – and it'll back up Laura's. We'll get everyone to do the swim." Debbie's eyes were alight with excitement and determination.

"Everyone?" asked Jack, puzzled.

"Yes, we've done it before. The water's

safe if you're not trying to swim against the tide. The whole of your class, the instructors, the teachers – everyone who can swim and wants to do it."

"There's safety in numbers," observed Jack grimly.

"Yes," said Debbie. "We'll get the buoyancy bags out of the dinghies and push them in front of us. That's what we did before. We had a race. It was great fun." She looked at them beseechingly. "We'll all get Jed home, won't we?"

"Only one drawback," said Jack.

"What's that?" asked Debbie.

"Suppose he doesn't show up?"

"He's on every tide," said Debbie. "Every single tide."

"But suppose we don't *see* him?"

"We'll see him," said Laura confidently. "I know we will."

ELEVEN

Debbie, Laura and Jack paddled back down the creek, dazed by the experiences they had shared and Debbie's brush with death.

The sense of shock stayed with them all the way back down to the Old Vicarage. The water, the blue sky above, the water meadows and the wheeling gulls suddenly seemed unreal and even sinister – as if the dark forces of Appelby's evil were even lurking in the wild flowers that ran down the bank to the creek. The eye of a cruising swan seemed particularly evil to Jack, Laura was momentarily terrified by the sight of a scarecrow on a ridge far away, and Debbie trembled quite visibly as a sudden, fitful breeze ruffled the water.

George and the other instructors as well as the teachers – and especially the children – thought a carefully supervised buoyancy bag race up the creek on the incoming tide was a terrific idea, and everyone was divided up into teams.

As they walked up to the estuary Jack whispered to Laura, "How do you feel?"

"Shattered," she pronounced gloomily.

"I mean – "

"You mean can I feel Ralph Appelby taking me over? No, but I'm terrified he will."

Jack noticed that beads of sweat were standing out on her forehead as if she had a fever. "You don't have to do this swim," he said, looking at her anxiously. "Why don't you stay on the bank?"

"I'm coming."

"But suppose – "

"I'm fighting him, Jack," said Laura grimly. "Fighting him all the time. He won't get in my mind that easily."

"Fighting who?" asked Naomi as she drew alongside.

"Nobody," said Jack quickly, but Laura was more careful. The last thing she wanted was to draw attention to herself, particularly when there was so much at stake for Jed.

"I'm fighting tiredness," she said. "We went for a long canoe journey with Debbie and it turned out I wasn't as good as I thought. I'm exhausted."

"So am I," said Jack, finding some tact at last. "We ought to have stuck with you lot."

Satisfied, Naomi ran on and Laura gave Jack a warning glance. "We've got to get him home," she said fiercely. "Whatever happens we've got to get him inside the Old Vicarage – to a place of safety. We've got to keep calm, Jack, and we mustn't let anyone suspect what's going on."

"They wouldn't believe us if we did tell them," grumbled Jack. Suddenly he was sick of the sound of Jed's name.

"Now listen everybody," said Debbie, standing in front of the whole group. They were all wearing bathing things and each team was armed with a large buoyancy bag. "Keep quiet – and do exactly what I tell you. When I say 'go', you'll all jump into the creek and hang on to your bags. Then I'll say 'go' again – and the leaders start pushing the buoyancy bags in front of them while the rest of you keep in line. The one at the back must be really strong, kicking out hard with his or her legs. Anyone who gets tired or short of breath must go to one of the stewards on the bank. The first team past the Old Vicarage wins."

Amidst much splashing and cheering, they soon set off. Jack and Debbie and Laura had all managed to be on the same team, and they pushed their buoyancy bag along with the swiftly moving tide. We'll scare him away with all this noise, Jack thought – we'll just scare him away.

For the first few minutes Jack was sure he would be proved right, and he condemned the whole idea as ridiculous. Then he heard Debbie say, "There he is!" And there he was – his dark head bobbing up and down, his arms cleaving the water as Jed swam between two of the teams.

"There *who* is?" panted Chris, and Tracy looked at Laura in surprise. Both were in their team and Laura wondered what Debbie would say to keep them quiet.

"Oh, just a friend," she gasped. "Come on, you lot, we want to win this!"

Jed kept them company all the way. Soon, Debbie's team were pulling ahead and Jed seemed to be swimming faster to keep up with them. Yet he never looked towards them, never acknowledged their presence, just kept ploughing through the water, carried along by the tide as he had been so many, many times before.

Slowly, the teams neared the Old Vicarage with Debbie's team pushing well ahead. And still Jed kept them company – and still Jed didn't look up.

As they neared the Old Vicarage, Jack began to worry that Jed would disappear

– that there was no chance of making the house at all. And directly he started thinking like that, Jed began to fall behind. Suddenly Jack realised that if he had negative thoughts Jed would be finished, and the only way of saving him was knowing they were going to do so – being totally positive about him.

Fiercely he set his mind to it, and he saw Jed begin to catch up with them again. Then, once more, he fell back and Jack knew that either Debbie or Laura was beginning to lose faith.

"We've got to think positive," he yelled at them, swallowing some water, choking and then spitting it out. "You mustn't think negative – either of you."

Immediately Jed caught up again and Jack knew that the others would think he was referring to the race.

Then, with a thrill of horror and apprehension, he saw that the Old Vicarage Adventure Centre was looming ahead. Could they keep Jed with them on the final fifty metres, or would Ralph Appelby have the last laugh after all?

With agonising slowness Debbie's team gradually neared the house. They were just ahead, Chris at the back kicking and pushing furiously, while the cheering of those on the bank reached new heights. Still the dark head was there, still Jed's strong arms cleaved the water – and still nothing happened to stop him.

Despite the frantic physical efforts, Laura was dizzy with fear, but she knew Jack was right – that they would have to be very positive. And in her case not only to move Jed on but to keep Ralph Appelby out.

"We're here," breathed Debbie. "And we've won!"

The cheering grew louder, and to their utter relief a boy dressed in a torn and ragged shirt and breeches dragged himself out of the water and stood up. He was as tall as Jack, strongly built with wide shoulders, and an anxious, exhausted face. But it was his eyes that were so incredible. None of them had ever seen such happiness in anyone's eyes before.

Very calmly, as if she was not in the least startled and without saying a word, Debbie took Jed's hand and helped him up the bank. He staggered a little as if totally

exhausted and then, without warning, Jed seemed to lose substance and Jack and Laura found they could see right through him.

"Come on," Debbie said quietly. "Come on, now. You're home – home at last."

It was the strangest sight as she led Jed towards the door of the Old Vicarage.

He looked almost translucent in the light streaming from the long windows, but Laura realised that everyone else was so euphoric after the race that they had not noticed Debbie and Jed at all. Wearing a dripping bathing costume, her hand held out – holding nothing as far as they could see – Debbie walked slowly inside.

As the door of the house closed Laura and Jack both knew that after so many weary tides, Jed had come home at last.